S0-DUS-155

A GIFT FOR:

....

FROM:

....

Copyright © 2012 Hallmark Licensing, LLC

Published by Hallmark Gift Books,
a division of Hallmark Cards, Inc.,
Kansas City, MO 64141
Visit us on the Web at Hallmark.com.

All rights reserved. No part of this publication may be reproduced, transmitted,
or stored in any form or by any means without the prior written permission of
the publisher.

Editorial Director: Delia Berrigan
Writer and Editor: Megan Langford
Art Director: Jan Mastin
Designer: Mark Voss
Lettering Artist: Sarah Cole
Production Designer: Dan Horton

ISBN: 978-1-59530-588-6
BOK1254

Printed and bound in China

MEMORIES & MESSAGES FROM A

grandparent

A FAMILY KEEPSAKE

CONTENTS

Dear .... *Morgan* ....,

We've had many conversations, but there are still many
stories I've never told you. Life keeps us busy, and I don't
always take the time to sit down and talk about myself.
I am giving you this book so you can read about those
stories and always remember them. After all, by learning
about my childhood, my education—even my hobbies
and role models—you'll understand how I became the
person—and the parent and grandparent—I am today.

Nothing in this world is as important as <u>family</u>, and I hope
that reading this book will give you a better understanding
of where you come from. Whether they make you laugh
or bring you to tears, may the memories and messages I've
written here bring us closer together.

Love,

.... *Gramma (Joyce Griffith Fox)* ....

Growing up is even more fun
when you do it with people
who love you.

Growing Up

MY FULL NAME IS:

....

MY FRIENDS CALL ME:

....

MY BIRTHDAY IS:

....

AS I WRITE THIS, I AM:

YEARS OLD

MY CHILDHOOD
NICKNAME WAS:

....

BECAUSE:

....

MY
FATHER

BORN:

MY
GRANDFATHER

MY
GRANDMOTHER

BORN:

BORN:

MY
MOTHER

BORN:

MY
GRANDFATHER

BORN:

MY
GRANDMOTHER

BORN:

MY DAD'S JOB:

....

....

MY MOM'S JOB:

....

....

A STORY ABOUT MY PARENTS
THAT I NEVER GET TIRED OF TELLING IS:

GRANDMOTHER, NANA, MEMAW . . .
THERE ARE MANY NAMES FOR GRANDPARENTS.

HERE ARE THE NAMES I CALLED MINE:

ONE THING
YOU SHOULD KNOW ABOUT
MY GRANDPARENTS:

....

....

....

....

....

I WAS BORN IN:

....

AND GREW UP IN:

....

OUR HOME LOOKED LIKE:

THESE ARE THE PEOPLE I LIVED WITH:

PEOPLE SAID I LOOKED JUST LIKE:

....

I ALWAYS THOUGHT I LOOKED LIKE:

....

A PERSON I ALWAYS LOOKED UP TO WAS:

....

....

....

....

....

I HAVE:

☐ SISTERS

☐ BROTHERS

I AM:

☐ OLDEST
☐ IN THE MIDDLE
☐ YOUNGEST

MY SIBLINGS AND I SPENT HOURS:

....

....

....

....

....

....

....

MY FIRST BEST FRIEND'S NAME WAS:

....

HERE'S HOW WE MET:

....

....

....

....

....

....

MY THREE MOST-LOVED
CHILDHOOD TOYS:

1. ....

2. ....

3. ....

ONE OF MY FAVORITE EARLY MEMORIES IS:

WHEN I WAS A KID,
ONE OF MY FAVORITE THINGS TO DO WAS:

....

....

....

....

....

....

....

EVERYONE THOUGHT
I WAS REALLY GOOD AT:

....

....

....

....

....

HERE IS SOMETHING THAT WAS
DIFFICULT FOR ME AS A CHILD:

I ALWAYS WISHED I WAS BETTER AT:

....

....

....

....

....

HERE'S HOW I EARNED MONEY AS A KID:

....

....

HERE'S HOW I SPENT IT:

....

....

WHEN I WAS LITTLE,
I WANTED TO GROW UP TO BECOME A:

....

....

....

....

....

....

MY FIRST CAR WAS A:

....

....

☐ LOVED IT ☐ HATED IT

BECAUSE:

....

....

....

....

THE **BEST PLACE** THAT CAR EVER TOOK ME WAS:

I CAN'T BELIEVE I USED TO WEAR:

....

....

....

MY FRIENDS USED TO TEASE ME WHEN I:

....

....

....

IF I COULD HAVE KEPT
ONE HAIRDO
FOR THE REST OF MY LIFE,
IT WOULD HAVE BEEN:

....

....

....

SOME OF MY CHILDHOOD
FAVORITE FOODS WERE:

- ☐ CHEESEBURGERS
- ☐ MEAT LOAF
- ☐ MASHED POTATOES
- ☐ FRIED CHICKEN
- ☐ SPAGHETTI
- ☐ FISH
- ☐ ....
- ☐ ....
- ☐ ....

ONE MEAL I WILL NEVER FORGET IS:

....

....

WHEN I WAS LITTLE,
MY FAMILY DESCRIBED ME AS:

☐ BRAVE

☐ KIND

☐ ADVENTUROUS

☐ LOVING

☐ CARING

☐ LOUD

☐ FUNNY

☐ ATHLETIC

☐ SHY

☐ OUTGOING

☐ ....

☐ ....

☐ ....

WHEN I WAS GROWING UP, I BELIEVED:

AS AN ADULT, I BELIEVE:

....

....

....

....

....

Those who seek both the knowledge found in books and the wisdom found in life get the best education of all.

Education

I ATTENDED ELEMENTARY SCHOOL AT:

. . . .

TO GET THERE, I:

- ☐ WALKED
- ☐ TOOK THE BUS
- ☐ RODE MY BIKE
- ☐ RODE IN A CAR
- ☐ . . . .

ONE REALLY FUNNY STORY ABOUT ELEMENTARY SCHOOL:

....

....

....

....

....

....

NOBODY SEEMS TO LOVE MIDDLE SCHOOL,
BUT FOR ME, THE WORST PART WAS:

....

....

....

....

THE BEST PART WAS:

....

....

....

....

....

IN HIGH SCHOOL, MY FAVORITE CLASSES WERE:

....

....

....

HERE ARE A FEW EXTRACURRICULAR ACTIVITIES I PARTICIPATED IN:

....

....

....

MY GRADES WERE:

☐ NOT SO GOOD

☐ GOOD

☐ VERY GOOD

☐ EXCELLENT

FOR FUN, I LIKED TO:

- [ ] GO TO CONCERTS
- [ ] SEE MOVIES
- [ ] GO TO PARTIES
- [ ] PLAY SPORTS
- [ ] ....
- [ ] ....
- [ ] ....

HERE ARE SOME UNFORGETTABLE
THINGS FROM THAT TIME:

MOVIES: ....

....

SONGS: ....

....

POLITICAL EVENTS: ....

....

TV SHOWS: ....

....

MY BEST FRIENDS WERE:

....

....

....

THE TEACHER
WHO MOST INFLUENCED ME WAS:

....

BECAUSE:

....

....

....

....

....

AFTER HIGH SCHOOL, I WANTED TO:

....

....

....

HERE'S WHAT I ACTUALLY DID
AFTER HIGH SCHOOL:

◯ MOVED AWAY FROM HOME

◯ WENT TO COLLEGE

◯ WENT TO TRADE SCHOOL

◯ PURSUED A CAREER

◯ ....

THOSE FIRST FEW YEARS
AFTER HIGH SCHOOL WERE:

....

....

....

....

....

MY COLLEGE YEARS WERE SPENT:

....

....

....

....

THREE PEOPLE
I MET IN COLLEGE WHOM I'LL NEVER FORGET:

1. ....

2. ....

3. ....

I CHANGED MY MAJOR [ ] TIMES
AND FINALLY DECIDED TO STUDY:

....

IN THE END, I:

◯ EARNED A DEGREE IN ....

◯ GRADUATED EARLY

◯ TOOK EXTRA SEMESTERS TO FINISH SCHOOL

⊠ NEVER GRADUATED

◯ ....

HERE'S HOW MY EDUCATION INFLUENCED WHERE I AM TODAY:

....

....

....

....

....

....

....

I'D LIKE TO LEARN MORE ABOUT:

....

....

....

....

....

....

....

Count your wealth in days well spent, in work well-done, in true and trusted friends.

Working Hard

MY FIRST JOB WAS: after school grade
working at my uncle Jam's dry cleaners
dr soda jirk at a soda fountain
clerk at a bakery and confectionary store
after grade 12 - assistant to the town
dentist.

WHEN I FIRST STARTED WORKING, I FELT:

nervous as I'd never answered

a Telephone. We didn't have

a telephone until I was 17 or 18 yr.

MY CURRENT JOB IS:

" DOMESTIC ENGINEER "

other wise known as housewife.

I'D DESCRIBE IT AS:

multi tasking with being
mother, grandmother, great
grandmother, wife.

HERE ARE THREE THINGS
I LOVE ABOUT WHAT I DO:

....

....

....

**HERE ARE THREE THINGS I WISH
I COULD CHANGE ABOUT WHAT I DO:**

....

....

....

IF I COULD START MY CAREER
ALL OVER AGAIN, I WOULD:

work harder at school

**IF I COULD DO ANYTHING
IN THE WORLD, I WOULD:**

Be a better parent

THE WORST BOSS
I EVER HAD TAUGHT ME:

....

....

....

....

....

....

THE BEST BOSS
I EVER HAD TAUGHT ME:

....

....

....

....

....

....

MY COWORKERS DESCRIBE ME AS:

1. TRUSTWORTHY
2. HARDWORKING
- PERPETUALLY LATE
- PUNCTUAL
- FUNNY
3. QUIET
- SMART
- STRONG
4. DETAIL-ORIENTED
- ....

Love

I FIRST FELL IN LOVE
WHEN I WAS:

....

I'LL NEVER FORGET:

....

....

MY FIRST KISS WAS WITH:

....

I'D DESCRIBE IT AS:

☐ ROMANTIC

☐ AWKWARD

☐ GROSS

☐ FUNNY

☐ ....

☐ ....

☐ ....

HERE'S THE STORY OF
HOW I MET MY BETTER HALF:

....

....

....

....

....

....

....

....

THREE THINGS
THAT FIRST ATTRACTED ME:

1. ....

2. ....

3. ....

TO ME, LOVE IS:

....

....

....

....

....

....

....

SOMETIMES, LOVE ISN'T EASY.
ONE THING I'VE LEARNED IS:

....

....

....

....

....

....

....

I GOT MARRIED ON ....

IN ....

THREE THINGS
I REMEMBER MOST ABOUT
MY WEDDING DAY:

1. ....

2. ....

3. ....

TO ME, MARRIAGE IS ALL ABOUT:

....

....

....

....

....

....

....

....

BEFORE I GOT MARRIED, **I NEVER THOUGHT:**

....

....

....

....

....

....

....

MY MARRIAGE IS:

- [ ] A PARTNERSHIP
- [ ] FULL OF GIVE-AND-TAKE
- [ ] SOLID
- [ ] ROCKY AT TIMES
- [ ] FUN
- [ ] FULL OF ROMANCE
- [ ] ....
- [ ] ....
- [ ] ....

CELEBRATED OUR ANNIVERSARY:

ONE OF MY
FAVORITE DATES WAS:

....

....

....

....

....

MY FAVORITE LOVE SONG IS:

....

....

....

IF MY LOVE LIFE
WERE A MOVIE, IT WOULD BE:

☐ A DRAMA WITH LOTS OF UPS AND DOWNS

☐ A LAUGHED-SO-HARD-WE-CRIED COMEDY

☐ A ROMANTIC COMEDY WITH A PERFECT,
HAPPILY-EVER-AFTER ENDING

☐ ....

IF I COULD TEACH YOU ONLY
ONE THING
ABOUT LOVE, IT WOULD BE:

....

....

....

....

It all comes down to this...
health, home, hard work,
family, friends, love.

Family

☐ I ALWAYS KNEW I'D BE A PARENT.

☐ I NEVER THOUGHT I'D BE A PARENT.

WHEN I FOUND OUT
I WAS GOING TO BE A PARENT,
I WAS:

☐ SHOCKED

☐ EXCITED

☐ THANKFUL

☐ OVERWHELMED

☐ ....

☐ ....

☐ ....

THE FIRST TIME I HELD MY CHILD
IN MY ARMS, I FELT:

....

....

....

....

....

....

....

WHEN I BECAME A PARENT, MY LIFE CHANGED FOREVER. HERE'S WHY:

....

....

....

....

....

....

....

OVER THE YEARS, I'VE LEARNED A LOT
ABOUT PARENTING. WHEN I FIRST
BECAME A PARENT, HERE ARE SOME
THINGS I WISH I'D KNOWN:

THE PARENTING MOMENT
I AM MOST PROUD OF IS:

....

....

....

....

....

....

RAISING A FAMILY IS:

- [ ] AMAZING
- [ ] CHALLENGING
- [ ] UNBELIEVABLE
- [ ] MY GREATEST ACHIEVEMENT
- [ ] ....
- [ ] ....
- [ ] ....

ONE OF MY FAVORITE
FAMILY MEMORIES IS:

....

....

....

....

....

....

....

MY MOST-LOVED FAMILY TRADITION IS:

....

....

....

....

WHEN MY CHILDREN WERE YOUNG, WHEN WE WANTED TO
DO SOMETHING SPECIAL TOGETHER
AS A FAMILY, WE WOULD:

. . . .

. . . .

. . . .

. . . .

HERE'S WHAT A TYPICAL DAY WAS LIKE
FOR US WHEN MY KIDS WERE LITTLE:

. . . .

. . . .

. . . .

. . . .

AT OUR HOUSE, BIRTHDAYS WERE:

☐ HUGE CELEBRATIONS

☐ NOT A BIG DEAL

☐ CELEBRATED WITH CAKE AND PRESENTS

☐ THE MOST FUN DAYS OF THE YEAR

☐ ....

☐ ....

☐ ....

THE BEST BIRTHDAY GIFT
I EVER RECEIVED WAS:

....

....

....

THE HOLIDAY I MOST LOOK FORWARD TO IS:

....

BECAUSE:

....

....

....

....

ON THAT DAY, WE ALWAYS:

....

....

....

....

....

....

I'M SO GLAD YOU TAUGHT ME TO:

....

....

....

....

....

....

....

....

HERE ARE SOME THINGS I HOPE YOU'VE LEARNED FROM ME:

- ☐ SOMETIMES IT'S OK TO BREAK THE RULES

- ☐ YOU CAN NEVER HAVE TOO MUCH LOVE

- ☐ YOU CAN BE ANYTHING YOU WANT TO BE

- ☐ IT'S IMPOSSIBLE TO STOP LEARNING

- ☐ ....

- ☐ ....

- ☐ ....

I'LL NEVER FORGET THE DAY YOU TOLD ME:

....

....

....

....

....

....

....

....

**GRANDPARENTS CAN'T HELP BUT GIVE ADVICE
TO THEIR GRANDCHILDREN.**

HERE'S MY ADVICE FOR YOU:

....

....

....

....

....

....

....

....

OUR FAMILY VACATIONS WERE:

☐ **NOISY**

☐ **BUSY**

☐ **RELAXING**

☐ **FUN**

☐ **SIMPLE**

☐ ....

☐ ....

☐ ....

MY FAVORITE PLACE TO GO WAS:

☐ THE BEACH

☐ THE MOUNTAINS

☐ CAMPING

☐ OVERSEAS

☐ HISTORIC SITES

☐ ON A ROAD TRIP

☐ ....

☐ ....

THINGS JUST WOULDN'T BE
THE SAME WITHOUT PETS.
HERE'S A FAVORITE STORY ABOUT MINE:

THREE WORDS
THAT DESCRIBE MY PET:

1. ....

2. ....

3. ....

*Time is measured by minutes
and hours, but life is measured
by memories and love.*

More About Me

HERE ARE A FEW OF MY
FAVORITE THINGS:

MOVIE: ....

SONG: ....

SPORT: ....

SPORTS TEAM: ....

FOOD: ....

TV SHOW: ....

VACATION SPOT: ....

BOOK: ....

AFTER A LONG DAY, HERE'S HOW
I LIKE TO RELAX AND UNWIND:

....

....

....

....

....

....

....

IF THERE WERE ONE CATCHPHRASE
I'D LIKE TO BE KNOWN FOR, IT WOULD BE:

MY PERSONAL PHILOSOPHY IS:

A FEW OF MY HOBBIES ARE:

- [ ] READING
- [ ] BICYCLING
- [ ] BAKING
- [ ] HUNTING
- [ ] KNITTING
- [ ] GARDENING
- [ ] FISHING
- [ ] COOKING
- [ ] GOLFING
- [ ] ....
- [ ] ....
- [ ] ....
- [ ] ....

IN MY FREE TIME, I LOVE TO:

....

....

....

....

....

....

....

MAKES ME FEEL PROUD.

I NEVER LEAVE THE HOUSE WITHOUT MY:

....

**SOMETHING YOU PROBABLY
DON'T KNOW ABOUT ME IS:**

....

....

....

....

....

....

....

THREE THINGS
THAT ALWAYS INSPIRE ME ARE:

1. ....

2. ....

3. ....

SOMETHING I'VE ALWAYS
FELT PASSIONATE ABOUT IS:

NOTHING HAS INFLUENCED
ME MORE THAN:

....

....

....

THE MOST DIFFICULT DECISION I EVER MADE WAS:

....

....

....

....

....

....

**AN INCREDIBLY INFLUENTIAL
PERSON IN MY LIFE WAS:**

My Dad. Daniel Lee Griffith

IF I COULD BE SURE THAT YOU LEARN JUST ONE THING FROM ME, IT WOULD BE:

....

....

....

....

....

....

....

....

IF YOU HAVE ENJOYED USING
AND SHARING THIS BOOK,
WE WOULD LOVE TO HEAR FROM YOU.

Please send your comments to:
Hallmark Book Feedback
P.O. Box 419034
Mail Drop 215
Kansas City, MO 64141

Or e-mail us at:
booknotes@hallmark.com